I am Your Daughter, Mam

JOANNE APPLEBY

STELLAR BOOKS

Published in 2019 by:

Stellar Books
1 Birchdale
St Mary's Road
Bowdon
Cheshire
WA14 2PW

W: www.stellarbooks.co.uk
E: info@stellarbooks.co.uk
T: 0161 928 8273

ISBN: 978-191-0275252

Cover by Katarina Nice
W: www.kitcatcards.co.uk
E: kitcatcards@gmail.com

CONTENTS

Mam, aged 21.

Dad, aged 21.

MAM VERSUS DEMENTIA

Do not think Dementia you have won.
You will not get a prize for being the
greatest thief of them all.
There are other tormentors who are
competing against you and will also wreak
havoc in their quest for supremacy.

Victory will be not be sweet but hollow.

You take the mind but not the heart and
the memories will always remain within
our hearts.

HOW DO I PROTECT

How do you protect when there's nothing
you can do?

How do you protect the very one who gave
birth to you?

How do you give the love she has given to
you?

How do you protect when there's nothing
you can do?

Looking at her now she's just a shell of
what she was.

And still the pain that rips you inside
remains firmly in place,
from that you cannot hide.

It's all over, but life still remains for them
it's confusion and nothing to be gained.

For me only the memories remain but they
are strong full of love and happiness too.

She took me to school and bought me an
apple or two

She waved goodbye at the bottom of the
school bank
now it's my turn to wave and not to look
back.

We've had a lifetime together Mam,
You made me who I am.
You loved me for who I am,
And you protected me.

And yes it's true I cannot protect you because I
am not a mother and you did what only mothers
can do.

THANKS MAM

A mother from the start.
You cried for me.
That still breaks my heart.

Your love has given me life.
I live each day with that inside me.

No one will ever know our bond.
No one will ever come close.

But inside I have a continuous ember that
glows in a winters chill.
I swim each stroke knowing somehow you
guide me.
For that I thank you Mam. You are
keeping me warm still.
On the dark lonely days the ember shows
me light.
On the dark lonely nights there is no chill.

You knew my life would not be easy and
have much pain to endure.
But my life has not been in vain
And the ember will always remain.

MY THOUGHTS ABOUT MY MAM

I have lost you
But you are still here.

You look the same, just a little older
Your eyes look at me and I know that you
can see me but there is only a stare, and a
silence that shows you have gone but you
are still there.

All we have now is the shadow of our Mam.
You are still the same but different.
You live without much knowledge that you
are still here.

You laugh and chat and even swear
without a care!

Whatever you are thinking wherever you
have gone, nothing and no one could ever
break our bond.

HOPELESSNESS

When nothing can be done,
What can you do?

When you don't have words,
What can you say?

Hopelessness touches everyone
No matter who they are, what they do or
where they live.

Hopelessness has no friends but it touches
everyone and everyone knows what it's like
to know hopelessness.

To feel it, is to know it.
To understand it, is seeing it right in front
of you.

To deal with it, is to turn and walk away
knowing the reason why you feel it is
because you care and have cared always.

Don't look back, there's no need.

ALONE

Dreaming through the night my thoughts
are consumed with illness.

Walking around the streets
The same thoughts are never far away.

I can't explain my feelings anymore.
I don't have any feelings anymore.

I exist only.

I feel still but everything else is moving
around,
the only sound I hear is your voice and the
simple words you use.

I am giving everything I can to
hopelessness,
it is taking everything and I give freely.

YOUR SOULMATE

You found your soulmate, Mam
You've been married 60 years
You found him at the local dance hall
You were both 18 years of age
He asked you to dance and you said yes
and history then was made.

You married three years later but had to
part National Service was a culprit but you
were in each other's hearts.

Finally you were back together and your
loving carried on 60 years down the line
your bond is still as strong.

Even though you don't have much
knowledge of who your sweetheart is
you still say his name over and over again
and ask where he is.

At times he's sitting right next to you and
still you do not know he is the man you
married all those years ago.

You still live in the village where you were
born. What a wonderful achievement to
have had a life in the little village.

Many people will never experience the
beauty you have had.

You were blessed with a beautiful voice and
played the piano too even now you still try to
play a little tune or two.

I remember when I was little girl I heard
you sing often,
I saw you sing at events and also weddings
too everyone in the village knew exactly
what you could do.

You do not sing these days
but that is okay Mam,
you shared that voice for many years and
now it's time to rest because when you
sang for all those years everyone knew you
were the best.

Life is cruel for many people for all sorts of
reasons.

And as I see you heading towards the end
of yours of course it breaks my heart.

But it also fills me with much admiration
for the simple country life you have led and
still lead.

This world now Mam is an awful place and in many ways I am pleased that you don't have to witness awful deeds that are spewed out by human beings.

And the awful diseases that sow their seeds.

I am your daughter, Mam.

Thank You indeed.

NO ANSWERS

As I watch you I cannot begin to
understand how evil appears to triumph
over goodness.

I watch you and all I feel is complete and
utter desperation.

Desperation at the fact that a beautiful
person has to endure the torture of
dementia.

There is nothing I can do.
There is nothing I can say.
Dementia has simply taken you away. And
has left you with the havoc that it scatters
along the way.

I hate myself because I sit and look at you
and there is nothing I can do and nothing I
can say that will release you from this
horrendous torture you endure every day.

DIGNITY

All I want to do is give you dignity now,
to give you back what you have given to me for
a lifetime.

I do not really know how to do that but
I hope I have.

It is a very strange feeling now,
I don't know what to say or do.
Hospital beds are arriving at the house next week
for you and dad.
That's the only way we can keep you at home.
You have been together sixty years,
only passing will part you.

I do not think, Mam you have any real
comprehension of what's going on,
maybe that is just as well.
Otherwise it would probably be a living hell.

Stay cosy Mam, in your little private world,
Enjoy your little sleeps, which are lasting longer
and longer now.

You are safe, warm and in your own home.
You will never be alone.

I promise.

16 DAYS

You lost your soulmate Mam but only for 16 days.
He went first to prepare a lovely setting to
welcome you in 16 days.
You passed Mam on 13th February 2019,
on the eve of Valentine's Day,

I think you and Dad had planned it all,
and you were to meet at the Gate,
and walk down the lane together.
Only 16 days out of 60 years you were apart
through no fault of your own.
Only illness was the culprit.

I have not lost you two, you both made me,
looked after me, raised me and loved me,
I ask myself how could I ever lose you two?
You are every fibre in my body, every breath and
step I take, from the moment I awake.

Once again you two are together,
enjoy it Mam and Dad.
Hold each other's hand, smile,
laugh in that lush meadow field,
I will feel you as the wind blows,
showing me gently as I go.

Neville sadly passed on 28th January 2019, aged 80.
With her dementia, Mam had no idea he had passed.
The one blessing of dementia is it saved her from a broken heart.

September 2018 enjoying a beautiful warm,
summers day overlooking her home village.

A WORD ABOUT DAD

My Dad was born on a farm in a small country Village in 1938.

He loved the farming way of life.
Unfortunately after his father passed the family could not remain in the farm and he moved to my mother's village in the late 1950s.

He met Mam at the local dance hall in 1956 and they married three years later.

My Dad was a very conscientious genuine hard-working man who always looked after his wife and family. He was devoted to my mother, a type of devotion sadly you don't see a lot of these days; they were also best friends.

Dad was only on the sick once in 40 years of being a self-employed builder. He fell off a ladder and broke kneecap and after rolling around on the floor in agony he went back up the ladder and fixed the spout he was working on he but then had to go home because he was in so much pain.   He didn't go to hospital; he preferred to put a bag of Birds Eye peas over the swelling on his knee-cap to see if that would help. Finally the next day he went to hospital. He had actually broken his patellar in two... as I said he was a very strong man! That accident happened on

Valentine's Day in 1999 he was back to work on May the 5th.

I was very lucky to have a Dad like mine; I went everywhere with him as a child. Every weekend we would go in the little mini-van visiting people on farms in the area. I learnt a lot from him and all those memories will remain with me forever.

Thank you Dad. For everything.

A WORD ABOUT MAM

My Mother was born in 1938 in the North East of England. She was the eldest of two daughters, born into a working class country family in the heart of a small country village.

Mam, was blessed with a beautiful, pure heart and soul. A real mother who adored children. She was also blessed with an excellent singing voice and was a talented pianist.

Throughout my childhood, I was fortunate to have a mother who was always there when I returned home from school or when I hurt myself and would go running to her. She protected me. To have a strong bond with your mother is a very special thing. And if you are fortunate enough to have this in your life, take care of it, make sure to look after her.

At the time of producing this book Mam was seeing her final hours out in her home with her family helped by Rothbury District Nurses, Alnwick Hospice Nurses and Macmillan Nurses.

Sadly on the day of the book being ready for print Mam passed away it was the 13th February 2019, only 16 days after losing Neville her husband and best friend of 60 yrs.

She simply gave up, she wanted to be with her lifetime Valentine. Together forever with her soulmate.

xxx

ABOUT THE AUTHOR

Joanne Appleby was born and raised in the North East of England.

She now resides in Manchester.

She wrote this book of poems as a tribute to her mother to repay a debt of gratitude, a mother who gave her everything and asked for nothing in return.

She can be contacted at joanne-appleby@hotmail.com

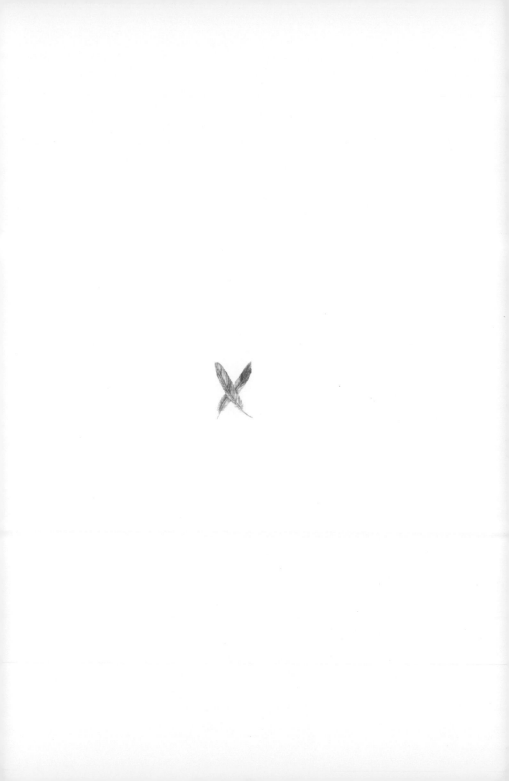